Echoes of the Heart

Carole Bergman

All poetry and illustrations by Carole Bergman

Copyright 2010 Carole Bergman
Printed by Lulu Press
All rights reserved.
ISBN 978-0-557-45930-8
This book or any part thereof may not
be reproduced without written permission from the publisher

For Ray

Table of Contents

Foreword .... vii-ix

Painting

Life's Journey 1
Circumstance 2
Love 3
Born Anew 4
Enchantment 5
Intangible 6
Afterglow 7
Enduring Love 8
Unbelieving 9
Eternal Hero 10
Almost Forgot 11
For Love's Sake 12
Love's Fire 13
This Dream Called Love 14
To My Beloved 15
Amazing Debt 16
Intoxication 17
Almost Missed 18
Camouflage 19
Crossroads 20
Ecstatic Dream 21
Love Shelter 22
Master Teacher 23
After the Loving 24
There Was One 25
Days of Love 26
Just One More Time 27
Pain Revisited 28-29
Amnesia's Lapse. 30
Devil's Weapon 31
Unwilling Player 32
On Stage 33

After 34
Invisible Escort.................................... 35
Avowal 36
Would I Had Met You.......................... 37
Answer 38

Painting

Ultimate Love...................................... 43
Tender Goodbye.............................. 44-45
Delayed for Love................................. 46
Facade.. 47
Rescuer.. 48
Because of Love.................................. 49
Sanctuary... 50
Precipice.. 51

Painting

Kate 55
Beekman Towers.................................. 56
New York 57
Christmas Present................................ 58

Painting

Dilemma.. 63
Live Now... 64

Foreword

These poems attempt to express the emotional nuances of my life and are written from the heart as the result of a lifetime of love, pain, and heartache.

While the poems of love were inspired by the man I loved and lost, others were inspired by my six children. And there are a delicate few that touch on the devastation of losing my son.

My history tells the story of me as an unwanted child. Born legally blind to an affluent family, I was the middle of three sisters and was rejected by each one of them. My mother gave me to a governess for the first three years of my life and from then on I was raised by housekeepers. My mother didn't want to take care of me and always reminded me that I was an accident.

Because my mother was ashamed of my disability, she was too embarrassed to let me wear glasses, even though the doctor advised I wear them at the age of two. I was indoctrinated into life with limited vision until the age of six, when the school insisted that I wear glasses. I learned to cope with my poor vision by feel, and, inadvertently, I learned to "see with my soul."

Fortunately, my refined aunts and uncles from my paternal side often visited because my grandmother lived with us six months of the year. They were extremely gifted and helped me appreciate the magic of language and the beauty of its creation. Uncle Lester recited Shakespeare and Keats and many other classical poets, teaching me the potency and power of words. I learned how essential they are in order for us to express our emotions, and how important they are in teaching us to cope with life's many challenges.

I started writing my own poetry at the age of eleven when I was extremely unhappy and was contemplating ending my life. I wrote frequently and feverishly whenever inspired or emotionally upset. Unfortunately, my mother did not accept my talent. She was furious that I showed a gift for writing when her favorite daughter did not, and called me a liar. I tried in vain to explain to her that I couldn't take the credit, as God and angels gave me the words. I wanted her love so desperately.

This is the poem I wrote at the age of fourteen trying to justify my writing to my mother:

Messenger

From God, to me, to you,
A messenger, that's all.
I really didn't write the words,
I just heard Heaven's call.
And maybe understood the words,
a little more than you.
But God and angels thought them up,
Believe me, this is true.
So I can't take any credit,
For writing words so fine.
God gave them me, to give to you,
To help make life divine.

Every poem I have written since then has been inspired by the love, the heartache, the tragedy and the suffering that has occurred in my life.

Poetry

Poetry is the language of the soul, the beat of the heart, the sensibilities enhanced by a sensitive nature to the thoughts, inspirations and experience of everyday existence.

Poetry is love, agony, ecstasy, heartbreak, despair, and all the varied emotions of the human spirit captured and shaped into something of enduring beauty.

Poetry is the deepest expression of self, the spontaneous exposure of the soul. To write poetry is to be in touch with your own soul, never letting the falsities and phoniness of life corrupt the truth within us all.

Poetry is the magic, the power, the beauty, and the music that ordinary words cannot express.

Poetry is the intense feeling, emotion and inspiration seized from our own life experiences and molded by the magic of words into word songs of deep meaning.

Poetry is observation, imagination, and visualization, set to the rhythm of our creation.

The language of poetry is condensed and must be listened to for overtones and suggestions as well as literal meaning.

The reader interprets poetry from a personal viewpoint and from the music of her own soul.

Life's Journey

Our lives have many avenues,
 Bridges, streets, tunnels and caves.
  A multitude of highways
   To lead us to our graves.

Some are brightly lit, some dark,
 Some need repair, some new.
  And yet there's not a single sign,
   One measly little clue

To tell us which will lead to joy
 Or which leads to despair.
  Not a hint of what's before us,
   When we should arrive there.

The smooth road could lead to sorrow,
 The rocky road to love.
  Still we must all travel blindly
   And trust in God above

That though we pick the roughest road,
 Our prayers won't be in vain.
  And hope the smooth road that we choose
   Will not lead us to pain.

Yet pray and struggle till we die,
 And travel on we must.
  Until the sands of time run out,
   And our souls turn into dust.

Circumstance

There is a true love on this earth,
 An unawakened heart,
  Who never might fulfillment find,
   Unless we do our part.

But tell me, what's the part we play?
 And how are we to know,
  The one God has molded for us,
   What marking will he show?

Will he be built a certain way,
 His eyes a certain shade?
  Will his voice have a certain ring,
   And he be a certain age?

Will bells peal out when he appears
 And life take on a glow?
  Will we be nearer Paradise?
  Oh how are we to know?

Or maybe like a flower,
 A seed is planted deep,
  Within our sweet subconscious,
   And only wakes from sleep,

Were love to lend a helping hand
 And open up our eyes.
  Yet sometimes, by a quirk of fate,
   We miss our Paradise.

Love

Love is not the sensuous or the strange
 The novelty of new lips pressing down
  Of clever hands that know how to caress.
   Love is not the words actors say.

Love is not the thrill I felt at first.
 Love is not your smile. Love's not your voice.
  Love is not a thing I ever had.
   Love is more precious than any other.

Love is not the lust, that is the least
 Love is not the satisfying end.
  Love is not the selfish or the small.
   Love is bigger than us all, beyond

A miracle of time and stars and space.
 Love is just a bit like being born
  Complete, with heart and soul
   And mind in place.

Born Anew

It was a magic moment,
 A fleeting, elusive dream.
  Just a moment's breadth of time
   Not meant to last it seems.

But in that brief ecstatic time,
 The heaven that I knew
  Erased my pain and heartaches,
   And I was born anew.

Alive, once more, able to express
 Love's passion and its bliss,
  Awakened to love's wonder
   By the magic of your kiss.

Enchantment

I shall remember
 This day as a dream
  A short glimpse of heaven,
   Far from the earth's scene.

I will remember
 This night as a spell
  That enwrapped me and kissed me,
   Had love words to tell.

I will dream of your kiss
 As only a wing
  Of an angel who touched my lips,
   Passing through spring.

I will remember
 Your arms with a blush
  Of soft sweet enchantment,
   I loved them so much.

I will remember
 The hours I knew you
  As a heavenly dream
   That I prayed would come true.

Intangible

There is something in me
 More than mortal when I am with you.
  More than pulse or breath or heartbeat
  Or anything I know.

There is something in me
 Surges like a liquor,
  When I look into your eyes.
  It courses down my middle vein

And sends a tingling through
 All my earthly shell.
  Calling, calling to each nerve,
   So that I can not bear

The throbbing ache of beauty that I feel.
 There is something in me that
  I never knew about
   Or thought about or yet can name

But maybe glimpsed perhaps in dreams
 I had forgotten to recall.
  On looking at the glaring dawn
   There is something in me like a song

That sings in silence, never ceases.
 Like a waterfall overlapping
  Itself again, again
   Cascading down a rocky cline.

There is something in me more than life
 More human, more than me myself
  Or poetry or words.
   There is something in me and will be,

As long as I am with you
 As long as you love me.

Afterglow

The glow isn't gone.
 It's a light all around
  My hair and my face.
   My feet won't touch the ground.

The glow isn't gone.
 The aura's still here.
  This soft shining light
   Just won't disappear.

I'm walking on clouds,
 See life through a mist,
  Since the moment we met,
   Since the moment we kissed.

I thought it would fade,
 Leave my heart, leave my mind.
  But it's grown more bedazzling.
   It's light leaves me blind.

I can't live without you
 Who knew you a day.
  But you're gone, and the magic
   Still won't go away.

Enduring Love

It must be wonderful
To be in love and not to be afraid.
Not afraid of time or foolish words,
Other people's thoughts, rumors or lies.
Darling, my love for you
They never could surmise.
It must be wonderful
To know the words you say
You mean today
And every other day.
Not to doubt or wonder if you'll be
Always so very much in love with me.
If maybe I should say a word awry
Or some word said amiss
Should hurt me and I'd cry.
It must be wonderful
To trust your heart and mind,
To see my imperfections and be kind.
Pass them over gently, smooth them down.
And with your loving kisses softly drown
The ache I have from knowing they are there,
Healed finally, beloved with your care.
Never to be lonely anymore
Just run to you and know that you'll adore me.
Though others turn away as well they might.
To no more fear the darkness of the night.
To long for it's deep solitude at last,
After the chaos of the day is past.
As one we'll melt in body for a time.
As always, dear, we are in heart and mind.
It must be wonderful
To look forward to life and love from you.
Oh, do you hear? It must be wonderful,
Marvelous and sublime,
To be in love and no more fear.

Unbelieving

Still I doubt such loveliness is true.
  Your smile, your arms, your kiss, I marvel yet.
You're here beside me, though you're free to go.
  My hands are wide, bars were not built for love.

I hold you softly, gently, close to me,
  A fragile thing, I dare not ever crush.
And still you say what I wish to hear,
  As if words I said had forced you to.

While I with wondering eyes can scarcely hide
  The giddiness your words can make me feel.
I dare not breathe or talk, I tremble so.
  One act amiss and all will tumble down.

Who would believe, I live a dream awake,
  Wading in mists, on carpets of soft clouds?
But surely I will wake one day to find,
  All is enchantment gained from loving you.

Yet you are here, I listen and I hark.
  But still I doubt such loveliness is true.

Eternal Hero

Because you gently hold my hand
 To walk life's paths with you
  Because you try with all your heart
   To make my dreams come true

Because you are my lover
 And yet my dearest friend
  Because it seems this love affair
   Will never ever end

Because we met and fell in love
 Only yesterday
  And you are still my hero
   There's only one thing I can say,
    "I love you."

Almost Forgot

Your loving me through all the years
 And always being there
  Almost makes my heart forget
   The unloved child in tears.

The little child who cried and prayed
 And wanted not to be.
  The rejected girl that no one loved,
   The girl I used to be.

Your love almost made me forget
 Her sobbing in the dark,
  Trying to prove she was of worth
   To ease her broken heart.

Your love and care and tenderness
 Almost made me forget
  Her hopelessness and misery,
   The pain she's feeling yet.

The little child I used to be,
 The sweet young girl I was,
  Made me forget the agony
   Because of your great love.

Remembering those hungry years
 The ravished child still moans
  That no one loved or cared at all
   When she walked all alone.

For Love's Sake

If I must lie, to save you hurt,
 Pretend, to save you care,
  Change the color of my soul,
   To keep you from despair

I'd lie and cheat and curse a saint.
 I'd paint my soul with scarlet paint,
  Take heartaches twice my share,
   And never let you know the cause.

With my heart bound in scalding gauze,
 I'd meet Hell's fiercest dare.
  And then I'd lie and lie again,
   Till my tongue cracked, my lips grew numb.

And only stop this grand farce when
 You are on Earth the happiest one.

Love's Fire

As you gently hold me to you
 And your lips caress my breasts,
  I can forget the pain and heartache
   And just recall the best.

I again thrill to the wonder
 Of a love that death defies
  As I raise my body to yours,
   For that rare breathtaking high.

And your strong yet gentle manhood
 Searches for its secret niche,
  To know once more the raging passion
   And the rapturous sweet relief.

And that ecstatic magic moment
 Of love's passion and desire,
  Unites our bodies rhythmically
   As we quench love's blazing fire.

This Dream Called Love

They wondered why I loved him
And I said, "Those of you who do not feel
This pulse of mine so quickly beating,
Cannot believe it so."
Something through the ages not defined
Is the explanation to this feeling I possess.
Not because of wondrous beauty.
Not because of treasures rare.
Not because of pity
Or the need for someone near.
But I've searched the wide world over
And I never hoped to find
Anyone but husband or lover
Not someone a saint to me!
My own brain is taxed and puzzled
And my heart is full, so full.
When I try to reason how I found my love,
The thrill of being his, always to know
The haven of love on earth,
Not to dream of the hereafter,
But to find here the ecstasy
And mirth of heaven, invisible angels sing.
My heart, though full, is light as spring,
And my mind refuses to ponder
Over things mere mortals wonder at,
This dream called love.

To My Beloved

My whole of life is you,
 Its reason and its why.
  My whole world lies within your arms,
   Release me, I should die.

With you each day is beauty
 The Spring shall never cease.
  I do not hear disharmony
   You are my whole of peace.

The years we spend together
 Shall never be enough.
  It seems I met you yesterday,
   I still thrill to your touch.

Your love is priceless treasure.
 Your presence fills my day.
  Your sweet regard must always
   Keep me half amazed.

I cannot find the reason
 You love me as you do.
  So I must wonder always,
   What magic did I do?

Amazing Debt

What do I owe to you my love
 Who gave me everything?
  Who taught to me the art of love
   Who made my Winter Spring?

Who helped me reach each mountain peak,
 And swim the roughest seas?
  I owe to you my very breath,
   The woman that is me.

Who tenderly nurtured my broken heart
 And brought it back to life?
  Who gave me Paradise on earth
   When you proudly called me wife?

I only owe you all I am,
 All that I'll ever be.
  You were the timber of my life.
   You gave me dignity.

Intoxication

Like whiskey
 The wonder of your arms.
  Like subtle thunder
   Your voice's charms.

Like a spring breeze envelops
 A cold young bird,
  Was your kiss that said
   What my heart just heard.

Almost Missed

I almost missed the beauty,
 The love, the ecstasy,
  Because of those who said
   You weren't good enough for me.

I almost listened to their lies
 The snobbery, disdain
  Of those who said my loving you
   Would only give me pain.

I almost believed their scandalous threats,
 Their dire prophesies,
  That money was your motive,
   Not great love for me.

I would have missed my whole of life,
 It's meaning and it's why,
  If I had listened and believed
   One tawdry little lie.

If the sheer intoxication
 Of your arms, your touch, your kiss
  Did not mesmerize my senses,
   I would not have known life's bliss.

If I had not been fearless
 And not braved love's awesome dare,
  I would have missed the magic
   Of a love beyond compare.

Camouflage

My life is less than a grain of sand,
  More dull than the hum of a bee,
    As fleet as the wind, as frail as a bird,
      When your love is not by me.

I see a sunset, I see a star.
  I hear the lark at dawn.
    And I know my breath will falter and fade
      If your tenderness is gone.

They look and they see a rounded soul,
  The mortals we meet and seek.
    But beneath the shell is the wounded heart
      Of a child who tried not to weep.

So come all ye mortals, laugh and be gay
  The child is hidden well.
    And I dance in the sunshine and love and play
      But the child must live in Hell.

Crossroads

Nary a clue to the fork I should take,
 Nary a sign to guide.
  Standing once more at the crossroads,
   I must choose, now's the time to decide.

The road to the left looks greener somehow,
 And the bend looks smooth up ahead.
  But the other promises flowers and song,
   Though the road be rough that I tread.

Oh what shall I do? Let a bolt from the blue
 Light up the road I should take.
  For one fatal step on the wrong road,
   And there's no way to change the mistake.

Ecstatic Dream

I don't expect to feel again,
 The passion of your kiss
  Or know once more the rapture
  Of your love and tenderness.

I don't expect to feel the magic,
 Rushing through my being,
  Touching all my woman's senses,
  Reawakening all my dreams.

It was too fast and wondrous,
 Too sweet a chemistry.
  I'll believe that I was dreaming.
  Did you hold and fondle me?

I'll force myself to just believe,
 It was an ecstatic dream
  Brought to life for a brief moment
  And not the great love it seemed.

Love Shelter

Never, never let me go.
 Hear me, hear my prayer.
  While yet your arms enfold me,
   Hold me, lest I disappear,

Into the space and vastness of time,
 Into the scourges of sin.
  You ask me, beloved, not to change,
   Help me, if I'm to win

Against the deceit of a tinsel world,
 The advice that cynics may give.
  But don't let me go to fight alone,
   Or I'll surely die, though I live.

Master Teacher

You were my wine and music,
 My sun, my stars, my dawn,
  My warmth when I was shivering,
   My solace when forlorn.

You were love's master teacher,
 The wind beneath my wings.
  My love, my life, my very soul,
   You gave me everything.

You showed me how to live and love,
 With cautious, gentle ways.
  Master teacher in the art of love
   Who gave me wondrous days.

You gave my life its reason,
 Showed me joys I never knew.
  Enchanted, rapturous, magic nights,
   Being loved by one like you.

You gave my world its meaning,
 My life its very worth.
  With you beside me as my love,
   You gave me heaven on earth.

After the Loving

I love my head when it's folded back
 From the pressure of your lips,
  And the touch of your hand caressing me
   While I'm lost in a dreamless kiss.

I love your smile when I stop to look
 At your flushed face after the thrill,
  And your tenderness and the aching hush
   And the longing for you still.

I love your moist lips as they fondle my breasts
 That spark the passionate ache of desire,
  And the magic spell that stirs my sense
   When that spark bursts into love's fire.

I love the thrill of our bodies pressed close
 As they fill up the ache in my soul,
  And the heaven I know in your embrace
   And this feeling that never grows old.

I love your strong manhood pressing my thigh
 Before our bodies are turned into one.
  The exciting instant of the breathtaking high,
   The soft fall when the loving is done.

I love the sweet contentment I feel
 Through the veins of my very being,
  When the beat of my heart goes faster, so fast,
   From the glow that our loving brings.

But in a word what I love most of all,
 Are your lips that caress like soft dew
  As you tenderly whisper, after the loving,
   Like a song, the words: "I love you."

There Was One

There was one who spoke a word
Hurt like a serpent's sting.
But I turned round the corner
And began a song to sing.

There was one who beat me
Till my heart and mind were sore.
But like the martyr that I was
I smiled and asked for more.

There was one who made a promise
He soon forgot to keep.
But in return, I closed my heart
And soon forgot to weep.

There was one who teased and taunted me
Till I scarce could catch my breath.
But as soon as I accepted him,
Spun on his heel and left.

There was one and two and three,
Four and five and six,
Who cut the scars upon my heart,
With lies and wiles and tricks.

But there was one, one all alone,
Loved me without a lie.
And 'tis for him, who loved me so,
I lie awake and cry.

Days of Love

All the days of love and caring
 All the days of wine and song
  They're over now, no more to be
   They didn't last for long.

All the days of happiness
 All the days of you and me
  Those magic wondrous rapturous days
   Never more on earth to be.

All the days of joy and laughter
 All the days of dreams come true
  All the days of love and wonder
   Since you're gone, they've all gone too.

Just One More Time

Just one more time to see your face,
Hear your voice and feel your touch.
Hold you close and feel again,
The thrill from loving you so much.
To feel your lips upon my own,
And know again the ecstasy
Of the miracle and wonder,
That your loving brings to me.
The fire and the fervor
The manhood that ever thrived,
The desire and the passion
And the love light in your eyes.
The magic thrill that ever grew
More potent with the years.
Through tragedy and heartache,
Through laughter and through tears.
I'd give my life to hear you say
"My darling, I love you."
I breathe, I talk, I smile, I walk
And yet my life is through.
Without you here beside me,
I am but an empty shell.
And although the sun is shining,
I am doomed to live in Hell.
If I only knew the reason
For your so sudden swift demise.
For the cruelty of your leaving me,
Before my very eyes.
For the purpose of my life now,
For the reason and the pain,
For the anguish I must still endure,
Because I still remain.
I need your love so desperately,
I pray my life will end
So I can be with you forever,
My precious lover, my best friend.

Pain Revisited

I saw the child of long ago
She looked a lot like me.
Her limpid eyes were glazed with pain,
From crying silently.
She had just about forgotten,
The girl who wished to die.
But now it all came back to her,
And she knew the reason why.
She was alone as she had been,
All of her life before,
Her hero came to rescue her
But he was here no more.
And the lashes she was taking,
From those she treasured so
Was something she was used to,
A long, long time ago.
The pain and the rejection,
She'd forgotten to expect,
Came back again in many ways,
A word, a look, a threat.
It was something she learned as a girl,
Before love changed her life,
Before she was valued and adored,
By one who named her "wife."
All the kindness and the caring,
Had traumatized her so,
She couldn't believe she lived this dream,
And the tears began to flow.
Cruelty didn't faze her,
She had lived with it so long.
Violent words didn't amaze her,
She was not meant to be born.
She wasn't supposed to be on earth,
She was told that constantly.
A crazy accident of birth,
She wasn't meant to be.
And all the years of all her life,
She was not allowed to sob

For beatings, blows and cruel words.
So it wasn't quite so hard.
But when a caring word was spoke,
Or she received a tender kiss,
She felt the hidden tears explode,
And fill the huge abyss.
And so she learned to comprehend,
Strange as the new fact was,
She was desired and adored,
And deserved the joy of love.
It took a while, she waited,
For the blows that never came,
Or the cruelty of the lashing tongue,
She was so used to pain.
But love and kindness took hate's place,
And violence turned to tenderness.
She almost perished from the beauty,
And the magic of love's bliss.
But all the time she half expected
The horror she'd always known,
Would conquer love and again haunt her
And she'd once more walk alone.

Amnesia's Lapse

I tried to make myself forget
 By dancing, laughing, loving, yet,
  Although my heart said, now you're free,
  That loving you was not for me,

An inner voice broke through the jest
 And said, you know you'll never rest.
  Your heart forgot not to remember
  The kisses warm, the words so tender.

I'd find another, then you'd see
 I did find one, who loved just me.
  But victory was empty gain.
  Inside my heart, the pain remained.

I tried, I tried to make believe
 And keep my heart not on my sleeve.
  I even tried to fool myself
   That memories were on a shelf,

The memories I had of you.
 But foolish, foolish heart you knew
  My love was still a flaming ember.
  My heart forgot not to remember.

Devil's Weapon

Dangerous weapons cruelly used
 To threaten, demolish and abuse
  A child's life, a woman's worth,
   Words, the most potent things on earth.

Once said can never be retrieved,
 But ever leave a soul to grieve.
  A force that leaves a mind deranged,
   To wander aimlessly in pain.

For lost dreams and love, now out of place
 Oh why do we let them escape?
  To vanquish love and conquer hope,
   Better to have a hangman's rope

Around my neck, and yet we still
 Say words that can destroy and kill.

Unwilling Player

I'm still playing life's grueling game
 Without a backup near.
  I'd like to throw my cards in,
   And finally disappear.

But even though I'm losing,
 I've got to play until the end.
  Life's game is cruel, the road is rough.
  I can't see beyond the bend.

Will another arrow pierce my heart,
 Causing me more pain?
  I want to leave, I want to go.
   Why must I still remain?

To remember all the beauty,
 Of the love that we once shared.
  A moment's breath, and then you left me.
  Alone, frightened and unprepared.

On Stage

Another day upon the stage
 Another act to play.
  To force a smile, hold back a sob,
   Find the right thing to say.

While underneath the hot tears burst,
 Invade my aching heart.
  An actor on the stage of life,
   I bravely play my part.

I hear the rumbling of the crowds,
 The constant noise, the hush.
  I want to scream, I want to shout,
   "I miss him, oh so much."

The show goes on, I play my role
 Pretend it's not so hard,
  To stand on stage and fool the crowd
   And scream and sob, but not out loud.

After

Life goes on among the ruins
 Of all that used to be.
  The grass still grows,
   The flowers bloom.
    The birds sing merrily.

All seems just as it was before.
 The sun comes streaming down,
  Nourishing all living things,
   Helping the world turn round.

And still my mutilated heart
 Perversely lingers on,
  Amidst the wreckage of my life
   Knowing joy's forever gone, is gone.
    Knowing joy's forever gone.

Invisible Escort

You were there tonight with me
  In every word.
In every thought profound and good
  Your sweet accord was heard.

You were sitting close by me
  Holding my hand in yours.
You were there tonight with me
  I know you were, because,

I heard you saying,
  "Be at peace with everyone around."
"Don't look for heartaches darling."
  "Enough of which you've found."

"Remember that I love you."
  "Don't ever be disturbed."
Yes, you were there tonight with me,
  And I was not afraid.

That's why I laughed and tossed my hair
  And spoke to everyone.
The love of you was everywhere,
  Although yourself was gone.

Your love kept me warm, safe, secure.
  Your love, your love, and nothing more.

Avowal

I will cleanse my heart of anger,
 Bitterness and vain regret.
  I will take the time allotted me
   To search for beauty yet.

I will not allow betrayals
 And cruelties of the past
  To strip my life of love's sweet beauty
   And joys that still can last.

I will close my heart to envy,
 Cruel lies and vile deceit,
  And take the strength still in my heart,
   To make my living sweet.

No more must my heart anguish,
 For the cruelty of lost years.
  Instead I'll pray for those who've hurt me
   Through my hot and teeming tears.

Every poison dart I've suffered
 Shall be as a growing change
  To show how hate and vengeance
   Can life's beauty disarrange.

I'll nurture all the love and kindness
 That was ever given me.
  And make each precious moment
   Last forever in my heart's sweet memory.

Would I Had Met You

Would I had met you dearest when I first opened my eyes
 Clear and green and sparkling before life made them wise.
  Would I had met you dear one when I was young and strong
   Quick to dream and fearless as lilting as a song.

Before I grew too old to think to dream of love was wrong.
 Before I learned a single day can be a lifetime long.
  Before my mirror reflected back disillusioned eyes.
   Before I learned of heartache before life made me wise.

Would my adored beloved I was kept brand new till when
 Your arms reached out to shelter me from all the wiles of men.
  And warm, safe and protected I lay content and calm
   Knowing with you loving me I'd never come to harm.

But fate had other plans in store, it seems I was to see
 All of pain and bitterness before you came to me.
  It seems I was to suffer all the torment and the trial
   Before you came and kissed me and taught me again to smile.

Would that beloved, we had met before all this was learned
 Before you had to soothe with love the heart that was so burned.
  But there was one saving factor for all that there was not
   My darling, that we met and loved before I had forgot.

Answer

Never trouble, never think
  Always on the bubbling brink
Of blazing immortality.
  Catch a dream, and wait and see.

Stand upon a cotton cloud
  Shout to Heaven, right out loud.
I'll be sinner, saint or king
  God or any mortal thing.

While the world is crying tears
  I'll go whirling through the years.
And all the petty worried band
  Who envy, but don't understand,

They'll scream and shout and curse their luck,
  Because they too, sank in the muck
Of time and trial and unsung dreams
  Of dead desires, unsolved schemes.

They didn't know the answer then
  But maybe when the world of men
Will hear their hearts and heed its call
  They'll realize, that love is all.

Ultimate Love

What must I do to spare you pain?
Tell me what shall I give?
I'd rake the scorching fires of Hell,
To give you your chance to live.

What must I do to give you years
Of any normal span?
I'd sell my soul to Satan
To have you grow to be a man.

What magic is there in my power?
What throbbing in my breast?
To see that you survive each hour
To see you pass the test.

How can I stop the tortures
You're forced to take to stay alive?
I'd rip the heart from out my breast
To see that you survive.

I'd gladly take the lashes,
The pain and torture too,
To keep you well, strong and alive,
There's nothing I wouldn't do.

Tell me quickly, tell me true
Tell me now and ever,
What can I do to make you well
And bound to leave me, never?

If caring were the potion
And unmatched love the cure,
You'd live life as you were meant to,
And be well forevermore.

Tender Goodbye

Forgive me, love, I must say goodbye.
You gave me wings and taught me to fly
You gave me songs to sing and poems that rhyme
But I must say farewell, it is now time.

Life holds for me only memories
Of things that were and now can never be.
I am not brave, but stood up fierce and proud.
Pretending to be strong, I fooled the crowd,

And though I cried, I never sobbed aloud.
So let me go, my love, you gave me much,
A lover's passion, and joys that I could touch.
You gave me all the happiness I knew.

Forgive me, dearest love, goodbye to you.
Forgive me, gentle one, I've cried too long.
I am a liar, I am not brave and strong.
I ache for him, and sob for him with pain.

I must go to be with him again.
Oh let me go, my love, do not be sad.
Know that you gave me all the joys I had.
You gave me nights of love and days of joy.

Forgive me, but I miss my baby boy.
Farewell, my love, for I have lived too long.
He wants to hear me sing his summer song.
I have to say goodbye, he needs me so.

Oh, little love, why did you have to go?
I must leave your sweet father to join thee.
Goodbye, dear love, our son is calling me.
I have to go, don't try to hold me here.

I've stayed so long, beloved, please be fair.
I could not mend our broken dreams, and so,
Goodbye, my gentle lover, I must go.
My heart is torn between our son and thee

But I must go, sweet lover, forgive me.
Your eyes are filled with pain, your head bent low.
No matter, gentle lover, I must go.
I hear him calling, how he misses me.

And I must heed his plaintive melody.
Let go my hand and free my broken heart.
I must go, now is the time to start.
Do not look at me with a face of woe,

Tender, gentle lover, I must go.
He is our son, he's calling for me now,
I must go and kiss his fevered brow.
Goodbye, my life, my love, I leave you now.

Farewell, my darling, I must say goodbye.
Forgive me precious lover, please don't cry.

Delayed for Love

Your kindness and your gentleness
  Touch my very soul.
    I want to turn and leave this world
      Because it's growing cold.

But then you hold me close to you
  And kiss my tears away.
    And I know for a certainty
      I cannot leave today.

Facade

To the world, I'm fierce and strong,
  Brave and unafraid.
    Only you my gentle love,
      My wracking sobs have heard.

And so I walk, my head held high,
  My steps seem strong and true.
    But I only live my life now,
      Because of one like you.

Rescuer

You pushed me back to life, the day we met.
I had learned never to hope, never to expect.
And, oh, the wondrous years we had,
The magic growing years.
When you taught me that life could be
More than a veil of tears.
We loved, we laughed, we worked,
We played, all this we did as one.
And then I saw the clouds
I'd known, part to let in the sun.
Happiness was something I could finally clutch
And hug close to my wondering heart,
And feel and know and touch.
My heart was full to bursting
With pure amazed joy, the beauteous day
That I gave birth to our beloved boy.
No ecstasy, no heaven above,
Could ever be so sweet as this,
Our earthly paradise.
Our life was now complete.
But then the clouds grew black.
The thunder roared and I knew then,
The fates I had ignored had come
To reap their vengeance on my joy.
They cracked my heart
And crushed my little boy.
I saw him struggle vainly to be free,
To live his life as it was meant to be.
He strove, he fought, he took
The greatest dare. I prayed,
I screamed to God to keep him here.
But all of my cajoling was in vain.
God took my precious baby just the same.

Because of Love

I'll stay here yet a little while.
 Your love will keep me here.
  And when I cry for our sweet son,
   You'll kiss away each tear.

I'll lie wrapped in your arms and dream.
 Your love will nourish me.
  Though I'll still think what might have been,
   I'll think what yet might be.

Sanctuary

When all my world is reeling
And my soul is scarred and sore,
I look for some safe haven
And I'm in your arms once more.
I sob, I cry, I shriek, I shake,
I wish that I could die.
But I cannot leave my gentle love
Or bear to make him cry.
So I pick up all the pieces
Of my bleak and battered world,
And try to patch them somehow
As I did when just a girl.
But the ache that's deep inside me
This time is here to stay.
And all my protestations
Won't make it go away.
The regrets that I have are real
And tear my heart and mind.
And I wish that it were in my power
To strike my memory blind.
So silently I weep inside
For our beloved son,
And know my world has shattered,
Before my life is done.
No tears, no shrieks, no pleading,
Can bring back my darling boy,
Or end the heartache that I feel,
Or give life any joy.
And my world won't stop its shaking
And my heart and mind are sore.
So I run to my safe haven
And I'm in your arms once more.

Precipice

On the edge of madness
I am forced to stay.
No one ever would suspect,
I'm sane in every way.
I laugh and talk with others.
I listen and I hear.
But underneath lies rumbling,
A million unshed tears.
So many times I've tried in vain,
To ease my grieving heart.
But it is terminally ill,
Since my world fell apart.
Sometimes for almost days on end,
I'm able to suppress,
The awful blight that scarred my soul,
And caused it to regress.
No one could ever start to know,
The tortures I endure,
Knowing in this lovely world,
My boy is here no more.
'Tis then I feel the madness,
Enveloping my being.
Wiping out all reason,
Causing me to scream.
And once again I'm left to face,
The most intense of sorrows.
And fervently, I wish that there
Will be no more tomorrows.
And while this madness stays with me,
I search for some sure way,
To ease my ravaged broken heart,
And take my life away.
But suddenly, the tide recedes,
And drenched, depleted, sore,
I am left to roam
The edge of madness evermore.

Kate

There were twenty thousand suitors
  Vying for the hand of Kate.
    There were twenty thousand suitors,
      But only four would wait.

And then the day grew cloudy,
  The sun was hid from view.
    By the time Kate had aspired,
      There were left but only two.

And then a dozen minutes
  Took Kate to make her mind.
    For who says in Never Never land,
      That love is always blind?

For one was short and stocky,
  And one was tall and slim.
    And neither was quite right for Kate
      Who wanted one more medium.

And so the day was almost gone
  'Fore Katherine could decide.
    By that time, there was only one
      Who'd take her for his bride.

So Kate grew cross, and stamped her foot
  And shed two tears, not one.
    And when the tears dried on her lids,
      She looked and there were none.

Beekman Towers

I looked down upon my city,
From on a roof top high.
I saw the cars, they crawled like ants,
Then lo, I saw the sky.
The sky was close and blue and clear,
With just a tinge of gray.
A dark ethereal midnight blue,
That soon would turn to day.
Day with all its pettiness,
With all its pain and strife.
Oh far, far, far more real you seemed
To me, cool soothing night.
I felt a part of sky and stars,
And moon and air, and joy.
And gazing on my city,
It seemed a child's toy,
That I could play with and control,
According to my whim.
Not cold and heartless, wide and vast,
Nor oh, so full of sin.
Sin and vice and lust and greed,
Crouching laying wait,
To spring on unsuspecting souls,
Deceasing them with hate.
And though I knew it could not be,
I prayed with all my heart,
With every atom of my being
That I could thus impart,
That night with all it's wondrous powers
Would never, never fade,
And like a monarch I could view,
My city unafraid.
But dawn would break and dreams
Would fleet and oh the dire pity–!
Would that I could find Paradise,
In my city, oh my city.

New York

A necklace strung across the sky
  Of softly curving lights
    All quite correct in unison,
     A beacon for dark nights.

Reflections on the Hudson
  Of life on Jersey's shore.
    The moon lighting a watery path,
     The ferry I adore.

The thrill, the loving of it all
  Will never dull, be gone.
    New York, the fairest of them all.
    New York, my home, my home.

Christmas Present

Fifth Avenue and Christmas,
 And you and I together.
  Lighted windows, Christmas Carols,
   The crisp and clear Yule weather.

Rockefeller Center
 And proud St. Patrick's steeple.
  Your protecting arm around me,
   The skaters and the people.

Our laughter as we walked along,
 My arm inside your own.
  The wondrous joy of loving you,
   And to no more walk alone.

Dilemma

And now that life is winding down
I still can't fathom why
Man is put upon this earth
to live, love, laugh, and die.
The excruciating agonies
We all must suffer so.
The brief elusive ecstasies
Most of us never know.
I can't perceive the purpose
For the heartache and the pain
The hopes we lose, the dreams that die
The love given in vain.
My whole of life I've strived and searched
To finally understand
Why we pay so high a penalty
For the price of being man.
Sometimes for a brief moment
I vaguely comprehend
The why to this dilemma
Then I'm confused again.
I can't explain the countless tears
The aim of every life
The method to this madness
The cause behind our strife.
It seems I live only to seek
And never ever find
The answer to these questions
That so besiege my mind.
Perhaps some broken heart would mend
Some life made less forlorn
If I could just discover
The reason man was born.

Live Now

And now I've learned to my dismay
 The moments simply do not stay.
  The days and weeks speed by so fast
   It seems that now is soon the past.

It does no good to look behind
 We cannot change the course of time.
  The only thing that's in our power
   Is to make the most of every hour.

With things to do and words to say
 Before the moments fade away.
  And leave regrets that make us cry
   "I should have" or "If only I."

Not take for granted what is here
 But live before days disappear.
  For time is something we can't keep
   And if we waste it we must weep.

The here and now is all there is
 So don't wait, now's the time to live.

Born and raised in New York City, Carole Bergman attended the Franklin Art Institute and Hunter College, while writing, publishing, and working as an illustrator and fashion designer in the garment industry.

Bergman has exhibited her work as a calligrapher and illustrator of Japanese Brush Painting in several one-woman art shows, and has also given poetry readings in schools, libraries, and art centers throughout Long Island, including Hofstra University and East Meadow High School where she was Poet-in-Residence in 1986.

Bergman has served as Artist-in-Residence at several schools and has been a member of the Town of Oyster Bay Rotational Art Exhibit for many years.

Her poems have appeared in various literary journals and anthologies including: *Towards Forgiveness*, Writers Ink Press, 2010; *Captured Moments*, National Library of Poetry Anthology, 1998; *Passionate Whispers*, National Poetry Forum, Dorrance Co., 1998; *Commemorating Excellence: The 1998 Presidents Awards*, National Authors Registry, Iliad Press, 1998.

The Lion's Eye Bank for Long Island at North Shore University Hospital gives the poem Bergman wrote for her eye doctor titled, "Thank you, Doctor," to everyone who donates a cornea to the eye bank.

Three of Bergman's poems about New York have won awards in competitions and two of her poems, "Healing Love" and "Avowal," have been auctioned at the World Trade Center to aid the victims.

Carole Bergman is the mother of six children, and lives in her Long Island home where she lived with her husband, Raymond, to whom this book is dedicated, until his death in 1993. This book is a testament to that marriage.

www.ingramcontent.com/pod-product-compliance
Lightning Source LLC
Chambersburg PA
CBHW041403020526
44115CB00036B/12